Quotations from Chairman Sam

Quotations from Chairman Sam

The Wit and Wisdom of Senator Sam Ervin

EDITED BY HERB ALTMAN

HARROW BOOKS
Harper & Row, Publishers
New York, Evanston, San Francisco, London

First HARROW BOOKS edition published 1973.

LIBRARY OF CONGRESS CATALOG CARD NUMBER: 73–14845

STANDARD BOOK NUMBER: 06–464002–7

To

Bern, Rene, Irv, Abbe, Sue, and Lisa.
Without them, so much would still be just a
pleasant daydream.

And with special gratitude to Emily Otten and
Nancy Cone for their indispensable help in
putting this together.

Contents

WHO IS SAM ERVIN?

The facts are readily available. You can have them for the price of a postcard. Facts dry as straw, prose that would delight a conscientious writer of obituaries.

BORN: Morganton, North Carolina, September 27, 1896

FAMILY: Married June 18, 1924, three children, seven grandchildren

EDUCATION: Graduate of University of North Carolina and of Harvard Law School

MILITARY SERVICE: Twice wounded and twice cited for gallantry in World War I. Awarded Purple Heart, Silver Star and Distinguished Service Cross

PUBLIC SERVICE: Associate Justice North Carolina Supreme Court, State Representative, U.S. Representative and U.S. Senator

LEGISLATION: Author or sponsor of Criminal Justice Act, 1964; Bail Reform Act, 1966; Narcotic Addict Rehabilitation Act, 1968; Bill of Rights for American Indians, 1968

AWARDS: Too numerous to mention

RELIGIOUS AFFILIATION: Elder in Presbyterian Church

Facts, but they won't tell you who Sam Ervin is. To find out you would need to know that it was he who, as a fledgling Senator, denounced the Wisconsin demagogue Joe McCarthy as a character assassin, while others stood by much as the three monkeys: seeing, hearing and speaking no evil. You would have to listen as he recited passages from Shakespeare, Kipling, Longfellow and the Bible, the words coming alive with meaning and truth. You would have to hear him caution our "King Richard" that "Divine Right went out with the American Revolution." You would need to look at his thumb-marked, dog-eared copy

of the Constitution, of which he knows every syllable, and which
he is never without.

You would have to see the shy grin stretch across his open face
and watch those horseshoelike eyebrows jiggle with delight as he
tells those homespun tales of his beloved North Carolina. You
would also have to observe that same happy face turn dark with
anger as he listens to an Erlichman imply that for all practical
purposes the Constitution is dead. The Constitution, which Sam
Ervin has called "the greatest thing to come from the mind of
man." You would have to hear him disarm an opponent by
telling him, "Why, I'm just an old country lawyer."

But probably the best way to find out who Sam Ervin is, is to
watch the young people. The young people who just a little while
back were chanting "don't trust anyone over thirty" have taken
to their hearts a seventy-six-year-old southern senator who has
somehow managed to bridge the heretofore unbridgeable generation and credibility gaps. These same young people who a short
time ago had turned their backs on a system they deemed un-
workable are now wearing Sam Ervin T-shirts. And the reason
for this is really quite simple. They have found in Sam Ervin a
how-to manual for making the system work. He has given them
courage and hope and direction.

Sam Ervin would blush at being placed in the ranks of Jefferson, Paine, Holmes, Thoreau, Darrow, and the handful of other
giants who fought the lonely fight for the rights of the individual.
But as history will surely show, he has earned his rightful place
alongside them.

Watergate

On June 17, 1972, five men were caught burglarizing and bugging the headquarters of the Democratic National Committee, located in the Watergate Hotel, in Washington, D.C. A search of the suspects produced several thousand dollars in hundred dollar bills, which were traced to the opposition party's Committee to Reelect the President. The burglars were brought to trial and subsequently convicted. However, before being sentenced, one of the five "sang," implicating the occupants of some of the highest offices of government, right up to the oval office in the White House. By unanimous consent of the Senate, the Select Committee on Presidential Campaign Activities was formed to investigate the charges. Senator Sam Ervin was to be its chairman. So began Act I of the most sensational political drama in this country's history, and it boasted a star-studded cast:

SENATOR SAM ERVIN, chairman—(D) North Carolina
SENATOR HERMAN TALMADGE—(D) Georgia
SENATOR JOSEPH MONTOYA—(D) New Mexico
SENATOR DANIEL INOUYE—(D) Hawaii
SENATOR HOWARD BAKER—(R) Tennessee
SENATOR LOWELL WEICKER—(R) Connecticut
SENATOR EDWARD GURNEY—(R) Florida

JAMES McCORD
BERNARD BARKER
EUGENIO MARTINEZ   }   The Burglars
FRANK STURGIS
VIRGILIO GONZALEZ

E. HOWARD HUNT   }   The Masterminds
G. GORDON LIDDY

JUDGE JOHN SIRICA   Trial Judge

and the supporting cast:

HERBERT PORTER—former scheduling director of Committee
  to Reelect the President

HUGH SLOAN—former treasurer of Committee to Reelect the
  President

JEB MAGRUDER—former deputy director of Committee to
  Reelect the President

MRS. E. HOWARD HUNT (deceased)—wife of convicted burglar

GERALD ALCH—former attorney for McCord

ALFRED BALDWIN—former FBI man and lookout for the
  burglars

SALLY HARMONY—former secretary to Liddy

JOHN CAULFIELD—former White House aide and employee of
  Committee to Reelect the President

ANTHONY ULASEWICZ—aide to Caulfield

JOHN DEAN—former counsel to the President

MAURICE STANS—former chairman of the finance committee
  of the Committee to Reelect the President

JOHN MITCHELL—former attorney general and director of the
  Committee to Reelect the President

FREDERICK LARUE—former assistant to Mitchell

RICHARD MOORE—special counsel to the President

HERBERT KALMBACH—former personal attorney to the President

ROBERT MARDIAN—former assistant attorney general and attorney for the Committee to Reelect the President

EGIL KROGH, JR.,—former aide to Erlichman and head of the "plumbers"

CHARLES COLSON—former special counsel to the President

DAVID YOUNG—former White House aide, member of the "plumbers"

JOHN ERLICHMAN—former number two presidential assistant

H.R. HALDEMAN—former number one presidential assistant

GORDON STRACHAN—former assistant to Haldeman

JOHN WILSON—attorney for Erlichman and Haldeman

DONALD SEGRETTI—accused of sabotage campaign against the Democrats

PATRICK GRAY—former acting director of the FBI

TOM CHARLES HUSTON—former aide to the President

RICHARD KLEINDEINST—former attorney general

ELLIOT RICHARDSON—attorney general

HENRY PETERSEN—assistant attorney general

RICHARD HELMS—former director of CIA

GENERAL ROBERT CUSHMAN—former deputy director of CIA

GENERAL VERNON WALTERS—former director of CIA

ARCHIBALD COX—special government prosecutor

ALEXANDER BUTTERFIELD—former White House aide

FRED BUZHARDT, JR.—special presidential counsel

RICHARD M. NIXON—President of the United States

The drama is not yet played out. Other players are waiting in the wings, and Act II is soon to begin.

I think that the Watergate tragedy is the greatest tragedy this country has ever suffered. I used to think that the Civil War was our country's greatest tragedy, but I do remember that there were some redeeming features in the Civil War in that there was some spirit of sacrifice and heroism displayed on both sides. I see no redeeming features in Watergate.

On May 17, 1973, eleven months after the Watergate break-i▮
the Ervin Committee opened its first public session. Speakin▮
about the men Senator Weicker had characterized as havin▮
"nearly stolen America," Senator Ervin remarked:

What they were seeking to steal was not the jewel▮
money or other property of American citizens, but some
thing much more valuable—their most precious heritage
the right to vote in a free election.

My colleagues on the Committee are determined to un▮
cover all the relevant facts surrounding these matters, and
to spare no one, whatever his station in life may be▮
. . . The nation and history itself are watching us. W▮
cannot fail our mission.

May 17, 1973

Our citizens do not know whom to believe, and many o▮
them have concluded that all the processes of government have become so compromised that honest gover-
nance has been rendered impossible.

May 17, 1973

came up here during Joe McCarthy days when Joe McCarthy saw a Communist hiding under every rosebush, and I have been here fighting the "no-knock" laws and the preventive detention laws and indiscriminate bugging by people who found subversives hiding under every bed. In this nation we have had a very unfortunate fear, and this fear went to the extent of deploring the exercise of personal rights for those who wanted to assemble and petition the government for redress of grievances.

June 14, 1973

From his opening statement of the hearings:

The founding fathers, having participated in the struggl
against arbitrary power, comprehended some eterna
truths respecting men and government. They knew tha
those who are entrusted with power are susceptible t
the disease of tyrants, which George Washington rightl
described as "love of power and the proneness to abus
it." For that reason, they realized that the power of public
officers should be defined by laws which they, as well a
the people, are obligated to obey; a truth enunciated by
Daniel Webster when he said that "whatever government is not a government of laws is a despotism, let it be
called what it may."

May 17, 1973

on the importance and necessity of the Committee's investigations:

I don't like the surgeon's knife, but sometimes a cancer comes, a cancer on the body politic, and has to be eradicated the same way.

April 15, 1973

Special Prosecutor Archibald Cox petitioned Judge Sirica to enjoin certain key witnesses from testifying publicly before the Ervin Committee. His motion was denied.

The American people are entitled to find out what actually happened without having to wait while justice travels on leaden feet.

n criticism that the hearings might prejudice upcoming jury
ials:

is more important for the American people to find out
ıe truth about the Watergate case than sending one or
wo people to jail.

ames McCord, convicted Watergate burglar, swore that his
ormer lawyer, Gerald Alch, promised that if he would plead
uilty at his trial, he would be granted executive clemency. Mr.
Alch denied the accusation, saying that he had taken a lie detec-
or test to prove his truthfulness. Senator Ervin responded:

think a guilty person who is calm can pass one without
ıny difficulty, and a truthful person who is nervous could
ass one with great difficulty.

As the hearings got under way, witness contradicted witness,
memories became dim, at times fading completely, and perjury
flowed like wine.

We could wind this up pretty soon if everyone would tell
what he knows, but if we continue to play hide and seek,
then it could take a while.

                                           June 4, 1973

Herbert Porter, a young, ambitious minor executive of the Committee to Reelect the President (CRP), admitted perjuring himself to cover up huge cash payments made to G. Gordon Liddy, convicted Watergate burglar. He offered as his reason for his illegal act, an unquestioning loyalty to the president. A saddened Sam Ervin softly chastised the young man, quoting from Shakespeare's *Henry VIII:*

"Had I but served my God with half the zeal I served my King, He would not in mine age left me naked to mine enemies."

So you think it is kind of normal . . . to destroy those records after five men are caught in an act of burglary with money that came from the committee in their pockets?

Spoken to Maurice Stans, who was the Chairman of the Finance Committee of the CRP. He admitted destroying records that contained the names of secret contributors to the Nixon campaign.

An organization which wants a place in history has no need of a shredder.

to Maurice Stans's contention that "these things" happen in politics:

You know, there has been murder and larceny in every generation, but that hasn't made murder meritorious or larceny legal.

Told to John Erlichman, number two presidential assistant who had arranged for Mr. Stans to issue a deposition rather than testify in person before the grand jury:

It's quite possible that if Stans had gone before the grand jury, some inquisitive grand juror might have broke this whole story in August 1972 and this nation might have been spared the agony it has gone through since.

August 6, 1973

The evidence thus far . . . tends to show that men upon
whom fortune has smiled beneficently, and who pos-
sessed great financial power, great political power and
great governmental power undertook to nullify the laws
of man and the laws of God for the purpose of gaining
what history will call a very temporary political advan-
tage. . . .

I came from a state . . . where they have great faith in the
fact that the laws of God are embodied in the King James
version of the Bible. And I think that those who participated in this effort to nullify the laws of man and the
laws of God overlooked one of the laws of God which
is set forth in the seventh verse of the sixth chapter of
Galatians. "Be not deceived; God is not mocked: for
whatsoever a man soweth, that shall he reap."

Spoken to Frederick Larue, wealthy assistant to John Mitchell,
director of the CRP. Larue has pleaded guilty to the charge of
obstructing justice and will be a witness for the prosecution in
upcoming trials.

Men love darkness rather than light because their deeds
re evil.

(*John,* 3:19)

To Herbert Kalmbach, who secretly raised funds that were used
o pay off the Watergate burglars, allegedly for their silence.

am just a country lawyer from way down in North
Carolina, and I probably make inquiries with a little bit
more vigor than some of these high-faluting city lawyers
do.

July 17, 1973

Asked if the president had questioned him as to what he knew
about Watergate, John Mitchell's answer was an incredible no,
not since their brief meeting on June 30th. Senator Ervin could
not resist the following observation:

Well, if the cat hadn't any more curiosity than that it
would still be enjoying those nine lives, all of them.

July 12, 1973

Herbert Kalmbach, as other witnesses had, qualified his answers
by repeating, "In retrospect, I would have. . . . or "If I had it
to do over. . . ." This prompted Senator Ervin's observation:

Some people, unfortunately, are lightning bugs; the
carry their illumination behind them.

July 17, 1973

To a witness's evasive response, "I have no specific recall," Senator Ervin whimsically inquired:

Do you recall it otherwise than specifically?

President Nixon maintained a stony silence about Watergate
despite the pleas of his staunchest supporters that he tell the
country what he knew. He finally relented, commenting that he
had broken his silence after learning of new "major develop-
ments" in the case. Senator Ervin arched his quizzically expressive eyebrows and said:

I don't know what he is talking about, but I'm glad that
he is talking.

One of the most crucial issues debated at the hearings, and as yet
unresolved, is that of the limits of executive privilege.

I am certain that the doctrine of separation of powers
does not impose upon any president either the duty or the
power to undertake to separate a congressional commit-

tee from access to the truth concerning alleged criminal
activities.

July 24, 1973

I have very different ideas of separation of powers from
those expressed by the president. . . . First, if it exists at
all, it only exists in connection with official duties. Sec-
ond, under no circumstances can it be invoked on either
illegal activities or campaign activities.

On administration claim of executive privilege:

Divine right went out with the American Revolution and
doesn't belong to White House aides.

The President of the United States, by reason of the fact
that he holds the highest office as the gift of the American
people, owes an obligation to furnish a high standard of
moral leadership to this nation and his constitutional duties, in my opinion, and undoubtedly his duty of affording
moral leadership to the country place upon him some
obligation under these circumstances.

July 24, 1973

In a speech to the Senate on the abuse of executive privilege, Senator Ervin used the president's own words and hoist him by his own petard.

In fact, if we look back to 1948, we find then-Congressman Richard Nixon protesting on the floor of the House that President Truman had withheld information from Congress. He opposed the proposition that Congress could not question a refusal by the President to provide information with these words:

"That would mean that the President could have arbitrarily issued an Executive order in the Meyers case, the Teapot Dome case or any other case denying the Congress of the United States information it needed to conduct an investigation of the executive department and the Congress would have no right to question his decision.

"Any such order of the President can be questioned by the Congress as to whether or not that order is justified on the merits."

June 18, 1973

Through the testimony of Alexander Butterfield, a former White House aide, it was learned that President Nixon had secretly taped all conversations that took place in his office and on his phone. The Committee requested specific tapes that could shed light on the involvement or noninvolvement of key witnesses in the Watergate cover-up.

Dear Mr. President:
Today the Select Committee on Presidential Campaign Activities met and unanimously voted that I request that you provide the Committee with all relevant documents and tapes under control of the White House that relate to the matters the Select Committee is authorized to investigate under S. Res. 60.

Letter to the president.

My hopes are great, my expectations small.

On whether Nixon would release the tapes.

This is a rather remarkable letter about the tapes. If you will notice, the president says he has heard the tapes of some of them, and they sustain his position. But he says he's not going to let anybody else hear them for fear they might draw a different conclusion.

                                        July 24, 1973

Comment on Richard Nixon's letter sent to the committee regarding the tapes.

Having been refused the tapes and documents, the Committee voted unanimously to subpoena the president for their release

I think this litigation is essential if we are to determine whether the president is above the law and whether the president is immune from all the duties and responsibilities in matters of this kind which devolve upon all other mortals who dwell in this land.

During the testimony of Robert Mardian, former attorney for the CRP, Senator Ervin was called to a pay phone and returned beaming with the news that the president was releasing the tapes to the Committee.

I am pleased to announce that Secretary Shultz has called me and asked, and advised me, that the president has decided to make available to the committee tapes of conversations which may have been with witnesses before the committee and which are relevant to the matters which the committee is authorized to investigate.

Twenty minutes later he learned that the phone call was a hoax. Saddened and embarrassed, Senator Ervin said:

It appears that a hoax has been perpetrated upon the committee, at least upon the chairman of the committee. It was an awful thing for a trusting soul like me.

I think that we have had an unfortunate thing of glorifying high officials lately, attributing all wisdom [to them]. And those of us who stay around the Washington scene find out that they are just like the rest of us, that they too have feet of clay.

July 29, 1973

"Face the Nation"

One scratch of the pen is better than the slippery memory of many witnesses.

July 29, 1973

"Face the Nation"

On the validity of the testimony contained in documents, as against contradictory spoken evidence of witnesses.

Nixon's aides agreed to testify in executive session, but not in a public forum.

What meat do they eat that makes them grow so great? I am not willing to elevate them to a position above the great mass of the American people. I don't think we have any such thing as royalty or nobility to let anybody come down at night like Nicodemus and whisper something in my ear that no one else can hear. That is not executive privilege. It is executive poppycock.

Despite the fact that we have the precedents of four presidents giving evidence to the courts or congressional committees, the Constitution didn't collapse, the office of the presidency didn't suffer, and the heavens did not fall.

July 29, 1973

"Face the Nation"

During John Dean's testimony he dropped a bombshell when he stated that the Nixon administration had compiled an "enemies list" of those who were in opposition to Nixon. The list, which

was constantly updated, indicated those people who should b
harassed by Internal Revenue Service audits and other method
by which the "enemies could be screwed."

Now here's a man listed among the opponents—the ene
mies—whose only offense is that he believed in the Firs
Amendment and shared Thomas Jefferson's conviction a
expressed in the Virginia Statute for Religious Freedom
that to compel a man to make contributions of money fo
the dissemination of religious opinions he disbelieves i
sinful and tyrannical.

Senator Ervin was referring to the president of the Nationa
Education Association whose name appeared on the "enemie
list."
P.S. He had voted for Nixon.

To John Erlichman:

The greatest decision that the Supreme Court of the
United States has ever handed down in my opinion is that
of *Ex Parte Milligan* which is reported in 4 Wallace 2, and
the things I want to mention appear on page 121 of that
opinion.

   In that case, President Lincoln, or rather some of his
supporters, raised a claim that since the Civil War was in
progress that the military forces in Indiana had a right to
try for treason a man who—they called copperheads in

those days, that were sympathetic toward the South—a civilian who had no connection with the military forces, so they set up a military commission and they tried this man, a civilian, in a military court, and sentenced him to death.

One of the greatest lawyers this nation ever produced, Jeremiah Black, brought the battle to the Supreme Court and he told in his argument, which is one of the greatest arguments of all time, how the Constitution of the United States came into being. He said that the people who drafted and ratified that Constitution were determined that not one drop of the blood which had been shed throughout the ages to wrest power from arbitrary authority should be lost. So they went through all of the great documents of the English law from Magna Carta on down, and whatever they found there they incorporated in the Constitution, to preserve the liberties of the people.

Now the argument was made by the government in that case that although the Constitution gave a civilian the right to trial in civilian courts, and the right to be indicted before a grand jury before he could be put on trial and then a right to be tried before a petit jury, the government argued that the president had the inherent power to suspend those constitutional principles because of the great emergency which existed at that time, when the country was torn apart in the civil strife.

The Supreme Court of the United States rejected the argument that the president had any inherent power to ignore or suspend any of the guarantees of the Constitution, and Judge David Davis said, in effect, "The good and wise men who drafted and ratified the Constitution

foresaw that troublous times would arise, when rulers
and people would become restive under restraint and
seek by sharp and decisive measures to accomplish ends
deemed just and proper, and that the principles of constitutional liberty would be put in peril unless established by
irrepealable law."

Then he proceeded to say, "And for these reasons,
these good and wise men drafted and ratified the Constitution as a law for rulers and people alike, at all times and
under all circumstances."

Then he laid down this great statement: "No doctrine
involving more pernicious consequences was ever in-
vented by the wit of man than that any of its provisions
can be suspended during any of the great exigencies of
government."

And notwithstanding that we have it argued here in this
year of our Lord 1973 that the President of the United
States has a right to suspend the Fourth Amendment and
to have burglary committed just because he claims that
the records of a psychiatrist about the emotional or mental state of his patient, Ellsberg, had some relation to
national security.

July 25, 1973

John Erlichman responded to most questions with long rambling
replies, prompting Senator Ervin to quote from Longfellow's, "A
Psalm of Life."

The only thing that I recognize is that,

> Art is long, and Time is fleeting,
> And our hearts, though stout and brave,
> Still, like muffled drums, are beating
> Funeral marches to the grave.

We have taken ten or fifteen minutes on this proposition.

July 26, 1973

Provoked by Erlichman's claim that the president had the right
to break and enter and burglarize in the name of national
security, Sam Ervin passionately responded:

The concept embodied in the phrase every man's home
is his castle represents the realization of one of the most
ancient and universal hungers of the human heart. One
of the prophets [Micah] described the mountain of the
Lord as being a place where every man might dwell under
his own vine and fig tree with none to make him afraid.
And then this morning, Senator Talmadge talked about
one of the greatest statements ever made by any states-
man, that was William Pitt the Elder, and before this
country revolted against the King of England, he said:

"The poorest man in his cottage may bid defiance to all the forces of the crown. It may be frail, its roof may shake, the wind may blow through it, the storm may enter, the rain may enter, but the King of England cannot enter. All his force dares not cross the threshold of the ruined tenements."

And yet we are told here today, and yesterday, that what the King of England can't do, the President of the United States can.

July 25, 1973

To Erlichman's lawyer, John Wilson, who angrily accused the Committee of withholding some documents:

Mr. Wilson, I might state that it appears by implication or intimation, at least from the president's letter, that this committee does not have all the documents it ought to have. It has not been able to get them, and we do not have any plumbers to go out and seek for them.

July 26, 1973

H. R. Haldeman, chief of staff in the White House, stunned the Committee with his admission that the president had allowed him to listen to the tapes that he (Nixon) had denied to the committee. Senator Ervin declared:

I am not saying anything's wrong. It just shows there has been a little, what we call in North Carolina, "canoodling together."

To Haldeman's lawyer who objected to laughter from the audience.

Mr. Wilson, I wish you would tell me some way I can keep people from laughing. I have heard [it], I don't approve of it, and I wish they would restrain themselves and I have tried to restrain them, but I have been told that the only thing that distinguishes humanity from a lofty attitude of disdain, called brute creation, is the fact that man laughs and brute creation does not. But I am going to request everybody to try to restrain their laughter, and it will help us proceed in a more orderly fashion.

                                                    August 1, 1973

Haldeman, as Kalmbach and Erlichman before him, claimed that the payments made to the Watergate burglars were for "humanitarian reasons."

I wasn't born yesterday. I've observed the political organizations a long time, and I have never yet seen a political organization that was an eleemosynary institution. But assuming that the Committee for the Reelection of the President was an eleemosynary institution, can you tell his committee why it picked out as objects of their eleemosynary concern, that they didn't select anybody except seven men who were accused of complicity in burglarizing and bugging the headquarters of the opposition political party.

August 1, 1973

As I understand from your testimony, you agree that Assistant Attorney General Petersen could excuse [Maurice] Stans from going before the grand jury and have him testify by deposition in private offices or public offices apart from the grand jury. Well, that troubles me a little bit because of my conviction that all men, whether they are princes or peasants, former cabinet members or just ordinary Americans, ought to be treated equal before the law.

Well, don't you agree with me that a grand juror could cross-examine Mr. Stans better than he could a piece of paper?

It has been my experience in my long practice of law, if you don't ask the right questions, you don't get the right answers.

August 6, 1973

To Richard Kleindeinst, former attorney general, August 6, 1973.

Spoken with typical southern charm and gallantry to a raucous, boisterous demonstrator who was being ejected from the hearing room:

Will the lady please desist from her conversation?

                                        August 6, 1973

Constitutional Rights

Our greatest possession is not the vast domain, it's not our beautiful mountains, or our fertile prairies, or our magnificent coastline. It's not our great productive capacity. It is not the might of our army or navy. These things are of great importance but in my judgment, the greatest and most precious possession of the American people is the Constitution.

From an address given at Davidson College in North Carolina.

The finest thing to come out of the mind of man or the experience of men.

Senator Ervin, on the Constitution.

I have always believed that the most precious value of civilization is the freedom of the individual.

If America is to be free, the government must permit her people to think their own thoughts and determine their own associations without official instruction or intimidation.

September 25, 1971

From a speech to the Association of American Publishers.

The Constitution in all its provisions looks to an indissoluble union composed of indestructible states.

Senator Ervin quoting from the Supreme Court decision *Texas v. White*, 1869.

I think, that apart from the faithful observance of the Constitution by the president, the Congress and the courts, our country has no protection against tyranny.

What may be the ultimate fate of the prisoner is of relatively minor importance in the sum of things. His role on life's stage, like ours, soon ends. But what happens to the law is of gravest moment. The preservation unimpaired of our basic rules of procedure is an end far more desirable than that of hurrying a single sinner to what may be his merited doom.

Ervin's statement while Judge of the Supreme Court of North Carolina.

The First Amendment is not so much for the brave; it is also for the weak of heart, or those who are placed in such economically vulnerable positions that they cannot afford to risk sanctions.

I hate the thoughts of the Black Panthers, I hate the thoughts of the Weathermen's faction of the Students for a Democratic Society. I hate the thoughts of totalitarians. I hate the thoughts of people who adopt violence as a policy, but those people have the same right to freedom of speech, subject to a very slight qualification, as I have.

"The basis of our government being the opinion of the people, the very first object should be to keep that right; and were it left to me to decide whether we should have a government without newspapers, or newspapers without a government, I should not hesitate a moment to prefer the latter."

February 16, 1973

Quoting Thomas Jefferson in a speech at Texas Tech. University.

Our founding fathers were wise enough to know that there is no way to give freedom of speech and press to the wise and deny it to the fools and the knaves. Certainly they did not intend for the government to decide who were the fools and the knaves.

Some government officials appear to believe that the purpose of the press is to present the government's policies

and programs to the public in the best possible light. They appear to have lost sight of the central purpose of a free press in a free society.

September 29, 1971

Alexis de Tocqueville in 1835, after observing the operation of American democracy, wrote that the press, despite its penchant for abuse, should not be restrained. "There is no medium," he said, "between servitude and license; in order to enjoy the inestimable benefits that the liberty of the press ensures, it is necessary to submit to the inevitable evils that it creates."

This is an eloquent and wise statement. You either have a free press or you don't. There is no middle ground— no room for qualification and no room for an officially sanctioned version of the truth.

February 16, 1973

If you don't think a television news show represents the truth, you can turn off your TV. If you don't think a magazine represents the truth, you can cancel your subscription. You have the right to expose yourself to whatever information you want. But to have the government prescribing what the truth is or limiting the information available for the citizen is contrary to the First Amendment.

February 16, 1973

Bias, like beauty, is largely in the eyes of the beholder.

February 16, 1973

None of us like to be criticized, but I've always taken the position that public figures ought to look on the news media as the psalmist looked on Jehovah, "Though thou slay me, yet will I praise thee." This country can only live as a free society if we have a full and free flow of information.

On freedom of the press.

I believe in a wall between church and state so high that no one can climb over it.

When religion controls government, political liberty dies; and when government controls religion, religious liberty perishes.

April 23, 1971

From an address in the U.S. Senate.

Every American has the constitutional right not to be taxed or have his tax money expended for the establishment of a religion.

March 13, 1968

For too long the issue of government aid to church related organizations has been a divisive force in our society and in the Congress. It has erected communication barriers among our religions, and fostered intolerance. And it will continue to do so while such federal financial assistance continues unaided by a judicial pronouncement as to its constitutionality.

Letter to *New York Times* from Sam Ervin, August 26, 1966.

. . . it [the Nixon administration] is the most repressive administration we've had since John Adams, who induced the Congress to pass the Alien and Sedition Acts in 1798.

Amidst the day's ringing rhetoric of "law and order," it too often appears that public officials and politicians do

more talking than acting to solve America's crime problem.

October 8, 1970

On the District of Columbia Crime Control Act:

A garbage pail of some of the most repressive, near-
sighted, intolerant, unfair and vindictive legislation the
Senate has ever been presented.

This iniquitous bill is an affront to the Constitution, and as
full of unconstitutional, unjust, and unwise provisions, as
a mangy hound dog is full of fleas. This bill might better
be entitled "To repeal the Fourth, Fifth, Sixth, and Eighth
Amendments to the Constitution."

March 29, 1970

In 1970, Senator Ervin expounded on the "no-knock" provision of the Omnibus Crime Bill:

A giant step in conversion of our free society into a police state.

The "no-knock" provision of this bill is a horrendous blow at the heart of a free society.

February 5, 1970

It would not mean using the keys of the king to open all the doors, but using the king's axe to break down the door and break the window.

January 25, 1970

In other words, in order to capture criminals, the law enforcement agencies must act criminally—a little law-breaking does wonders for law and order.

May 10, 1973

"If the government becomes a lawbreaker it breeds con-
tempt for law; it invites every man to become a law unto
himself; it invites anarchy. To declare that in the administration of the criminal law the end justifies the means—
to declare that the government may commit crimes in
order to secure the conviction of a private criminal—
would bring terrible retribution. Against that pernicious
doctrine this court should resolutely set its face."

May 10, 1973

Quoting Justice Brandeis.

Thousands of citizens are confined each year, not because they are guilty of commission of a crime, but because they cannot afford to post bond.

January 23, 1965

On bail reform.

. . . it would remove the inequity of allowing pretrial
liberty to hinge on the accused's financial means.

September 16, 1965

On bail reform bill.

he real answer to the problem of crime committed by
ersons on bail, and, indeed, the solution to the general
roblem of crime, lies not in the preventive detention of
ndividuals presumed innocent, but in the speedy trial of
he accused and the swift and sure punishment of the
;uilty.

October 16, 1969

The SACB is a relic of the time when McCarthyism ran rampart in this great nation, when many people thought they saw Communists hiding under every bed and behind every rosebush.

The Justice Department and the Federal Bureau of Investigation are quite able to protect America from those who would attempt to overthrow her government by unconstitutional means. We do not need the SACB to stigmatize any individual or group which might be intelligently or politically obnoxious to the established order.

The courts have found most of the Board's functions under the Internal Security Act of 1950 to be unconstitutional, and as a result thereof, the SACB has had virtually nothing to do except draw its breath and salary.

Senator Ervin is an ardent and persistent foe of the Subversive Activities Control Board.

Computers in government make just as many errors as computers in industry, and the results can be infinitely more harmful than a bad credit rating.

November 19, 1970

Unless we take command of the new technology, we may discover some day that the machines stand above the law.

Regardless of the purpose, regardless of the confidentiality, regardless of the harm to any one individual [that might occur if there were no computer files], the very existence of government files about how people exercise First Amendment rights, how they think, speak, assemble and act in lawful pursuit, is a form of official, psychological coercion to keep silent and to refrain from acting. With the "total recall," the permanence, the speed and the interconnection of government data files rests the potential for control and intimidation that is alien to our form of government and foreign to a society of free men.

February 3, 1970

At this point in time it had become public knowledge that the federal government was amassing personal data on millions of American citizens and storing this information in computerized data banks.

When people fear surveillance, whether it exists or not, when they grow afraid to speak their minds and hearts freely to their government or anyone else, then we shall cease to be a free society.

On data banks.

Displaying a 1,245 page Bible that was reduced to a 2″ strip of microfilm, Senator Ervin said:

Someone remarked that this meant that the Constitution can be reduced to the size of a pinhead. I said that I thought that is what they had done with it in the executive branch because some of those officials cannot see it with their naked eyes.

February 24, 1971

If we are going to be a free society the government is going to have to take some risks. They can't put everyone under surveillance.

On data banks.

is my belief that while the Recording Angel drops a tear
ccasionally to wash out the record of our human iniqui-
es, there is no compassion to be found in any comput-
rs, nor is it to be found in all the new instruments for
reasuring man which the behavioral sciences and the
ew technology hold out for us.

June 21, 1971

On data banks.

Senator Ervin said that personality testing of Peace Corps volun-
teers called for true and false answers to statements that were an
invasion of privacy. Among the questions Ervin quoted were:

	TRUE	FALSE
My father was a good man.	___	___
I am very seldom troubled by constipation.	___	___
I like poetry.	___	___
I believe in the Second Coming of Christ.	___	___
I like to flirt.	___	___
I wish I were not bothered by thoughts about sex.	___	___

New York Times, September 24, 1966.

The lie detector is the primitive test of medieval times.
The lie detector will soon take its place with the ordeal
by water and the ordeal by fire. I think there is no place
in the American constitutional system for the use of twen-

tieth century witchcraft to determine if a man is fit for th
job.

Senator Ervin said the government had sufficient inve:
tigative resources to determine if a person is a securit
risk without strapping an applicant to a machine an
subjecting him to salacious questioning. Among the que:
tions were, "When was the first time you had intercours
with your wife?" "Did you have intercourse with he
before you were married?" "How many times?" The FB
does not use personality tests or polygraphs on applicant
for employment. I fail to see why the National Securit·
Agency finds them fascinating.

                                                    October 18, 1966

On lie detector tests given to applicant for a job with the Na
tional Security Agency.

There is not a syllable in the Constitution that gives the
federal government the right to spy on civilians.

Disputing assertions by the military that investigations of civilians were limited to those who demonstrated a penchant for
violence or other illegal conduct, Senator Ervin said:

It was enough that they* opposed or did not actively support the government's policy in Vietnam or that they disagreed with domestic policies of the administration, or that they were in contact or sympathetic to people with such views.

The army investigated these men during their campaigns for office and while they were in office.

December 17, 1970

On the army spying on civilians.

Too often in the Congress, as well as in the nation, there is an unwillingness to protect the privacy of our fellow men when they are of different political persuasion, different economic status or different mode of life. Until Americans learn to distinguish tyranny in any form, until each of us has the courage to protect the other man's privacy, we shall not be truly free.

*Senator Adlai Stevenson and Governor Otto Kerner.

Stories and Sayings
of a Country Lawyer

Spoken in a soft Carolina drawl, his stories—a blending of the Bible, the classics and the homespun philosophy of his beloved hill country—have made Sam Ervin the most avidly quoted raconteur in the U.S. Senate.

A witness before Senator Ervin's committee was trying to minimize his role in a flagrant graft operation. Senator Ervin told this story.

Jim had been killed accidently and his administrator was trying to hold the railroad responsible for the death on circumstantial evidence. He testified, that while walking the railroad track just after a train had passed, he had seen Jim's severed head lying on one side of the rail and the remainder of Jim on the other. The lawyer snapped, "What did you do after discovering these gruesome relics?" Well, the witness replied, "I said to myself, something serious must have happened to Jim."

June 13, 1958

Address to the American Bar Association.

Speaking against banning the teaching of evolution in the public schools:

Only one good thing can come of this. The monkeys in the jungle will be pleased to know that the North Carolina legislature has absolved them from any responsibility for humanity in general and for the North Carolina legislature in particular.

One time I was holding court and a man wanted to be excused from the jury panel on the grounds that he was deaf in one ear, and I said, "We will wait to see whether you will be selected to be on a grand jury, because a grand jury only hears one side of the case."

New York Times Magazine, May 13, 1973.

I am one of the few men in public life who doesn't complain much about his treatment at the hands of the press. The press takes me to task every once in a while, but they have always been very kind, not attributing my hypocrisy to bad motives. They have always attributed it to a lack of mental capacity.

When, during a session of the Watergate Hearings, Senator Baker remarked that Senator Ervin's law degree had come from Harvard with honors, Senator Ervin replied:

Thank God, no one would ever suspect it.

This teacher went into her classroom about fifteen minutes before the class was supposed to begin work and caught a bunch of her boys down in a huddle on their knees in the corner of the room. She demanded of them what they were doing, and one of them hollered back and said, "We are shooting craps." She said, "That's all right, I was afraid you were praying."

Congressional Record, January 12, 1967.

One time when I was presiding over a murder trial in Burke County, they had special veniremen summoned in from another county to make sure that the accused got a fair hearing. I asked one of these jurors if he could be fair, and he answered: "I think he is guilty of murder in the first degree, and he ought to be sent to the gas chamber. But I can give him a fair trial."

Military Justice Hearings, 1966.

I'd have to meditate a long time on a voluntary witness. The only other voluntary witness I've had is a man who calls me several times a week to tell that the Lord has communicated with him on Watergate. I advised this caller I would be awful glad to have the Lord come as a

witness but that I could not permit the caller to testify
because it would amount to presenting hearsay evidence.

April 19, 1973

On reports that Martha Mitchell was eager to appear before the
Committee.

Senator Ervin said that Senator McCarthy was charged
with being guilty of disorderly conduct by flyblowing.
That is a strong Anglo-Saxon word, but a very expressive
one.
It was explained that flyblowing was a word often used in the
South and that it meant "to smear."

New York Times, November 16, 1954.

In 1954, Sam Ervin, junior senator from North Carolina, was
appointed to the Select Committee to Investigate Censure
Charges against the late Senator Joe McCarthy.
Senator Ervin tells the story that Senator McCarthy reminds
him of Uncle Ephraim and the Lord.

There was a big religious meeting in the south mountain
section of the state. All the elders of the congregation rose
and told what the Lord had done for them, all but old
Uncle Ephraim Swink. Uncle Ephraim was bent, battered
and crippled by the years, and when the moderator

finally asked Uncle Ephraim, "What has the Lord done for you?" "He mighty nigh ruint me," said Uncle Ephraim. And that's what Senator McCarthy has done for the Senate.

November 15, 1954

I believe in clinging to the tried and true landmarks of the past, but I am willing to test the soundness of new ideas.

Bill asked his friend George, "What became of your old hound dog?"
He said, "I sold him for $5,000."
Bill said, "George, you know you never got $5,000 for that old hound dog."
He said, "No, I did not get it in cash, but I got it in trade. I took two alley cats which were estimated to be worth $2,500 apiece."

Voting Rights Hearings, 1965.

Asked about his political ambitions, Senator Ervin, who is seventy-six, laughingly replied that he was:

the only Democrat in the Senate who isn't suspected of harboring any plans to be President of the United States.

John Mitchell's claim that had he to do it over, he would have acted differently, prompted this story from Senator Ervin.

There was a girl down in North Carolina who had been "dishonored" by a rich man. The girl's father, rifle in hand, confronted the rich man.

"You have dishonored my daughter," said the angry father.

"But I am a rich man," said the accused. He promised to pay for his indiscretion—$15,000 for a baby boy, $10,000 for a girl.

"What if my daughter has a miscarriage?" demanded the father. "Will you give her another chance?"

Mr. President, the argument of my good friend from Maine that what this amendment is designed to accomplish has already been accomplished by the Byrd amendment reminds me of the story of the man in a distant part of the country who received a telegram from an undertaker informing him that his mother-in-law had died. The telegram of the undertaker closed with the inquiry, "Shall we cremate or bury?"

The man wired back and said, "Take no chances. Cremate and bury."

Congressional Record, August 11, 1967.

once knew this preacher back home who liked to use words that he sometimes didn't quite understand. One time he brought in a visiting preacher, and after introducing him to the congregation he told him to preach loud, "because the agnostics in this church are not very good."

Time Magazine, April 16, 1973

One occasion the following question was put to Dr. Hale: "Doctor, when you pray as Chaplain of the Senate, do you look at the tragic condition of the country and the many problems existing in the country and then pray that the Almighty will give the Senators the wisdom to deal with those problems and to find their solutions?"

In reply to that interrogation, Dr. Hale said: "No, I do not look at the country and pray for the Senators. I look at the Senators and pray for the country."

Congressional Record, January 26, 1966.

I've always been able to sympathize with what Jonah [in the Biblical story] is reputed to have said after three days: "If you'd kept your mouth shut, this thing wouldn't have happened."

Senate Airpower Subcommittee Hearing, 1956.

A North Carolina school committeeman informed his neighbor that the school board had decided not to renew for an additional year the contract of the man who taught science in the high school. The neighbor expressed his surprise at this action of the board, stating that he understood that this particular teacher had attended many colleges and earned many degrees. The school committeeman replied: "That's the trouble with him. He has been educated way past his intelligence."

May 21, 1963

Letter to Professor O'Neal.

Thomas Jefferson asked George Washington why the convention had created the Senate, instead of reposing all legislative power in the House of Representatives. Washington replied: "The convention created the Senate in order that it might do the same thing that your saucer is doing. You are cooling off your hot coffee in your saucer. The Constitutional Convention created the Senate in order that the hot legislation passed by the House might be cooled before it is poured down the throats of the people of America."

Congressional Record, February 5, 1963.

There is this man who is known as the most ignorant man in Burke County, North Carolina. Somebody once asked him if he knew what country he lived in, and he answered flat out, "nope." They asked him if he knew the name of the state, and he again answered, "nope." Well, they then asked if he had ever heard of Jesus Christ. "No," he answered. Finally, they asked if he had ever heard of God. "I believe I have," he said. "Is his last name Damn?"

Time Magazine, April 16, 1973.

I am possessor of a great affliction, a Scotch-Irish conscience, which will not permit me to follow after a great multitude to do what I conceive to be evil.

Newsweek Magazine, February 19, 1973

Throughout history, rulers have invoked secrecy regarding their actions in order to enslave the citizenry.

Open and full disclosure of the governing process is essential to the operation of a free society.

Awhile ago there were three lawyers together, and one of them bet another five dollars that he did not know the Lord's Prayer. So each one of them put up five dollars with the third one. Then they called on this lawyer to recite the Lord's Prayer, and he said, "Now I lay me down to sleep . . ." and the other lawyer said, "Go ahead. Pay him off. I didn't think he knew it."

Literacy Test Hearings, March 1962.

A ranking government official, evading specific answers on foreign aid spending, confined his answers to general statements. Ervin said:

The witness reminds me of the husband back home who told his lawyer he wanted to divorce his wife. He conceded that she was beautiful, a fine cook and a model mother. "Why do you want to divorce her," the lawyer asked. "Because she talks all the time," was the reply. "What does she talk about?" "That's the trouble, she never says."

May 25, 1957

There is an old story that illustrates the reluctance which characterizes all of us in certain areas. A gentleman, who was rather prominent in his community, attained his ninety-fifth birthday anniversary. On that day the newspaper reporters came around to interview him. And one of them asked how old he was. He said, "This is my ninety-fifth birthday anniversary." And the reporter said, "Well, you have lived a long, long time and have seen many changes in your life." And he said, "Yes, and I was against every one of them."

Hearings on American Indians, August 1961.

The truth often comes to a biased witness as the image of a rod to the beholder through the water, bent and distorted.

I once jokingly mentioned that the day may come when we will replace politicians with computers. Judging from some of the reasoning of politicians I've seen over the years, I know I would sooner take the logic of a computer. The machine may suffer the same lack of intelligence as some politicians, but at least there is consistency in its idiocy.

Washington Post, August 1973.

There was a young lawyer who showed up at a revival meeting and was asked to deliver a prayer. Unprepared, he gave a prayer straight from his lawyer's heart: "Stir up much strife amongst the people, Lord," he prayed, "lest thy servant perish."

Time Magazine, April 16, 1973.

A labor official appearing before a senate rackets inquiry was giving evasive answers. Ervin said that he reminded him of his boyhood visits to the carnival.

One concession had an employee who put his head through a hole in a hanging canvas and tried to dodge baseballs thrown at his skull by the customers. Baseballs were three for a nickel, and for each hit the customer won a prize. "I'd like to make arrangements to make you my dodgerman," said Senator Ervin, "because nobody would ever hit you, and everything would be clear profit."

June 2, 1958

To a witness confusing contradictory testimony, Senator Ervin told of a Carolina justice of the peace confronted with a difficult civil suit.

"After hearing the plaintiff the justice of the peace turned to the defendant and said, "I would appreciate it very much if you would not present your case because when I hear both sides it gets me confused, and I have trouble making my mind up who's right."

New York Times, June 23, 1959.

Fellow back home named Josh Billings said, "It is better to be ignorant than to know what ain't so."

Civil Rights Hearings, 1959.

I ask for more information because I am unable to un-screw the unscrutable.

March 15, 1960

Debate with Senator Dirksen.

I find that an apt story is worth an hour of argument.

If Senator McCarthy believed those things when he said them about the Senate Committee then there is a pretty solid ground to say that he ought to be expelled from the Senate for moral incapacity. If he put those things in there honestly believing them to be true, then he has evidently suffered gigantic mental delusions, and it may be argued with much force, that he should be expelled from the Senate for mental difficulty.

Senator Joseph McCarthy said that the Committee, of which Ervin was a member, in its reports, had imitated Communist methods.
New York Times, November 15, 1954.

It reminds me of Aesop's fable about the wolf and the lamb. The wolf was seeking an excuse to devour the lamb. So the wolf said to the lamb, "You are muddying the water in the stream from which I am drinking." The lamb replied, "I don't see how I could be muddying your drinking water. You are drinking upstream and I am drinking downstream." The wolf's reply was to gobble up the lamb. The moral of the fable, as given by Aesop, was that any excuse will serve a tyrant.

Congressional Record, March 14, 1964.

"Free people, remember this maxim: We may acquire liberty, but it is never recovered if it is once lost."

Quoting Jean Jacques Rousseau.

. . . the conduct of some teamster bosses makes Atilla the Hun appear to be a very mild mannered and benevolent individual.

Senate Rackets Investigation, 1958.

We had a man down in my state that did not agree with anybody about anything. He found that cabbage didn't agree with him, and thereafter he wouldn't eat anything but cabbage.

Civil Rights Hearings, 1957.

When I hear people talking about our sins and what they do to us, I am reminded of the story of a prominent citizen who lived to be ninety-six years of age. On his ninety-sixth birthday the newspapers sent their reporters out to interview him. One of them asked, "To what do you attribute your long life?"

The old man replied, "I attribute it to the fact that I

have never taken a drink of an alcoholic beverage or smoked a cigarette in all my days."

At that moment they heard a noise in an adjoining room that sounded like a combined earthquake and cyclone. One of the newspaper reporters said, "Good Lord, what is that?"

The old man said, "That is my old daddy in there on one of his periodic drunks."

Congressional Record, March 4, 1964.

I think after the election Nixon got such a tremendous vote, why he thought he had a great mandate from the people. In my judgment, he overlooked the fact it was not because they loved Caesar more, but Brutus less.

New York Times Magazine, May 13, 1973.

I would suggest there are two books that should be in the White House to read. One is the Constitution of the United States and the other is Dale Carnegie's book *How to Win Friends and Influence People*.

New York Times Magazine, May 13, 1973.